HOW TO DRAW VAMPIRES,
GHOSTS AND OTHER HALLOWEEN HORRORS

Mark Bergin

BOOK HOUSE

SALARIYA

Published in Great Britain in MMXII by
Book House, an imprint of
The Salariya Book Company Ltd
25 Marlborough Place, Brighton BN1 1UB

3 5 7 9 8 6 4 2 1

Please visit our website at **www.salariya.com**
for **free** electronic versions of:
You Wouldn't Want to Be an Egyptian Mummy!
You Wouldn't Want to Be a Roman Gladiator!
You Wouldn't Want to Be a Polar Explorer!
**You Wouldn't Want to Sail on a 19th-Century
     Whaling Ship!**

Author: Mark Bergin was born in Hastings in 1961.
He studied at Eastbourne College of Art and has
specialised in historical reconstructions as well as
aviation and maritime subjects since 1983. He lives
in Bexhill-on-Sea with his wife and three children.

Editor: Rob Walker

PB ISBN: 978-1-907184-66-6

A CIP catalogue record for this
book is available from the
British Library.

Printed and bound in China.
Printed on paper from
sustainable sources.

**WARNING: Fixatives should be
used only under adult supervision.**

Visit our websites to read interactive
free web books, stay up to date with
new releases, catch up with us on
the Book House Blog, view our
electronic catalogue and more!

www.book-house.co.uk
Information books
and graphic novels

www.scribobooks.com
Fiction books

www.scribblersbooks.com
Books for babies, toddlers and
pre-school children.

Follow us on Facebook and
Twitter by visiting
www.salariya.com

PER FROM
**SUSTAINABLE
FORESTS**

Contents

Making a start

Learning to draw is about looking and seeing. Keep practising and get to know your subject. Use a sketchbook to make quick drawings. Start by doodling and experimenting with shapes and patterns. There are many ways to draw but this book shows only some methods. Visit art galleries, look at artists' drawings and see how your friends draw, but above all, find your own way.

You can practise drawing figures using an artist's model — a small wooden figure that can be put into various poses.

When drawing from photos, use construction lines to help you to understand the form of the body and how its parts relate to each other.

4

Practise sketching people in everyday surroundings. This will help you to draw faster and train you to quickly capture the main elements of a pose.

Try sketching friends and family in creepy poses at home.

Perspective

If you look at a figure from different viewpoints, you will see that whichever part is closest to you looks larger, and the part furthest away from you looks smaller. Drawing in perspective is a way of creating a feeling of depth – of suggesting three dimensions on a flat surface.

The vanishing point (V.P.) is the place in a perspective drawing where parallel lines appear to meet. The position of the vanishing point depends on the viewer's eye level.

V.P.

Two-point perspective drawing

V.P.

V.P.

Two-point perspective uses two vanishing points: one for lines running in one direction across the figure, and the other for lines running in the opposite direction across the figure.

Three-point perspective drawing

Three-point perspective
drawings use three vanishing
points. This method is good
for drawing a figure from a
more dramatic angle.

V.P. = vanishing point

7

Drawing materials

Try using different types of drawing papers and materials. Experiment with charcoal, wax crayons and pastels. All pens, from felt-tips to ballpoints, will make interesting marks — try drawing with pen and ink on wet paper for a variety of results.

Silhouette is a style of drawing that uses only a solid black shape.

Ink

Charcoal is very soft and can be used for big, bold drawings. Ask an adult to spray your charcoal drawings with fixative to prevent smudging.

You can create special effects in a drawing done with **wax crayons** by scraping parts of the colour away.

Felt-tip

8

Pencil

Hard **pencil** leads are greyer and soft pencil leads are blacker. Hard pencils are graded from 6H (the hardest) through 5H, 4H, 3H and 2H to H. Soft pencils are graded from B, 2B, 3B, 4B and 5B up to 6B (the softest).

Pastels are even softer than charcoal, and come in a wide range of colours. Ask an adult to spray your pastel drawings with fixative to prevent smudging.

Ink

Lines drawn in ink cannot be erased, so keep your ink drawings sketchy and less rigid. Don't worry about mistakes as these lines can be lost in the drawing as it develops.

9

Creating characters

Creating a scary character can be a great deal of fun. Different characters and features can all be created from the same basic starting point.

Basic head construction

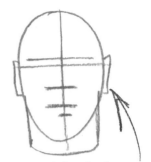

Draw in an oval head shape and mark in the position of facial features with construction lines.

Frankenstein's monster

Vampire

Devil

Grim Reaper

Zombie

Witch

Vampiress

Ghost

Try to see how many different characters you can create from your imagination.

Draw in a basic hand shape with straight construction lines.

Here are a few examples of how scary monster hands can be created from the first template.

Accessories:

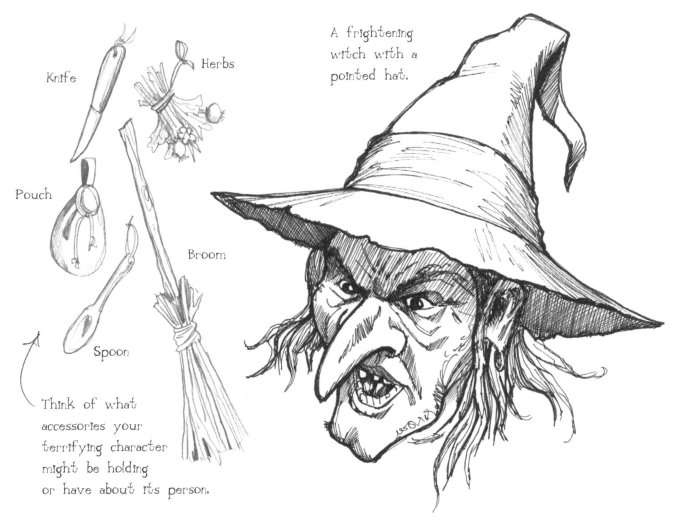

Knife

Herbs

Pouch

Broom

Spoon

Think of what accessories your terrifying character might be holding or have about its person.

A frightening witch with a pointed hat.

Drawing movement

You can make your drawing much more dynamic by giving it a sense of movement.

Start by drawing stick figures in action poses.

These can be the basis of your drawing showing where each limb is according to the position of the body.

A jumping ghoul

This ghoul is mid-jump. You can see how this pose is developed from the stick figure shown.

This finished drawing gives a sense of action. Adding movement lines around the drawing gives it a sense of momentum. The horse's mane and tail also fly out behind it as do the billowing clothes of the Grim Reaper.

Vampire

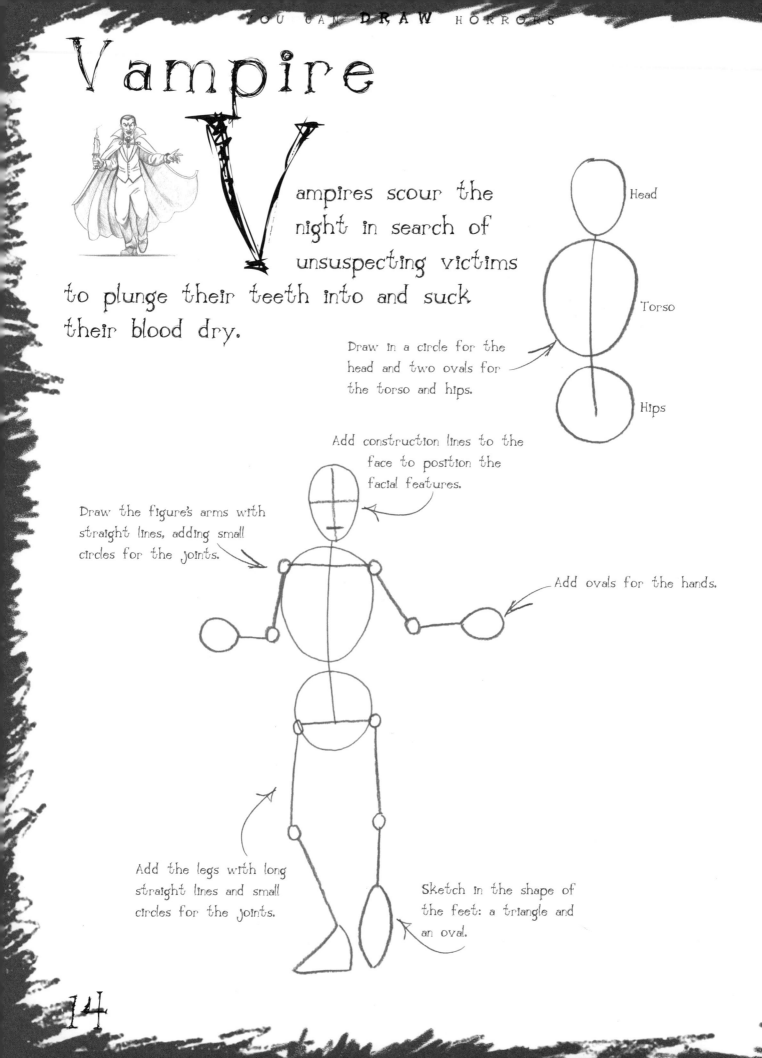

Vampires scour the night in search of unsuspecting victims to plunge their teeth into and suck their blood dry.

Head

Torso

Hips

Draw in a circle for the head and two ovals for the torso and hips.

Add construction lines to the face to position the facial features.

Draw the figure's arms with straight lines, adding small circles for the joints.

Add ovals for the hands.

Add the legs with long straight lines and small circles for the joints.

Sketch in the shape of the feet: a triangle and an oval.

Draw a simple candle in the vampire's hand.

Sketch in the facial features using the construction lines as a guide. Add the V-shaped hairline.

Add fingers to the oval hand.

Sketch in the shirt, adding cuffs and collar.

Draw the cape and collar using flowing curved lines.

Add the waistcoat and trousers with simple lines.

Complete the details of the face. Add tone to the hair and the mouth.

Draw in the chain using circles.

Add details to the candle and hands.

Add shading to areas light wouldn't reach.

Add buttons and details to the waistcoat.

Draw long curved lines for folds in the cape.

Finish the detail on the shoes.

Use an eraser to remove any unwanted construction lines.

Zombie

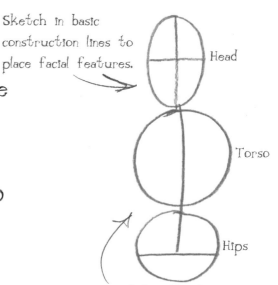

The 'dead' have risen and are walking the earth! The zombies will not stop until they have killed you and made you one of their own.

Sketch in basic construction lines to place facial features.

Head

Torso

Hips

Draw an oval for the head and two circles for the torso and hips. Join these with a centre line.

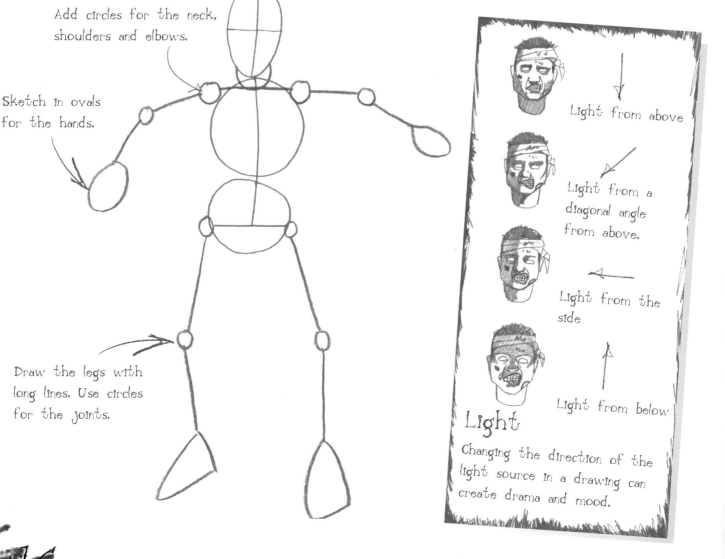

Add circles for the neck, shoulders and elbows.

Sketch in ovals for the hands.

Draw the legs with long lines. Use circles for the joints.

Light from above

Light from a diagonal angle from above.

Light from the side

Light from below

Light

Changing the direction of the light source in a drawing can create drama and mood.

Start to sketch in the facial features.

Add the jacket and shirt around the figure using the construction lines as a guide.

Add a belt.

Add fingers to the hands.

Draw the trousers around the legs.

Finish the face, making it as scary as possible.

Add detail to the shoes.

Draw holes in the flesh with bone showing through.

Draw in the details of the jacket, adding rips and dirt marks.

Add shade to areas light doesn't reach.

Complete the details of the trousers.

Remove any unwanted construction lines with an eraser.

Ghoul

Ghouls haunt graveyards or any other place that dead human flesh can be found. They devour the rotting meat, leaving nothing but the bones.

Draw a long oval for the head.

Head

Torso

Draw circles for the torso and hips.

Draw a curved line for the bent spine.

Add construction lines to the head to place the facial features.

Position the arms using lines and circles for the joints.

Sketch in ovals for the hands.

Add long lines for the legs and circles for the joints.

Draw in the creature's large feet.

Sketch in the basic facial features.

Add in the creature's wild hair.

Sketch in the basic shape of the muscle structure.

Add long claw-like fingers to each hand.

Draw in the creature's ragged clothes.

Add curved lines to create the shape of the legs.

Add toes to the feet.

Complete the facial features, giving special attention to the eyes and mouth.

Finish the wild hair.

Use tone to define the muscles.

Complete the sharp claws.

Add more lines and tone to the ragged clothes.

Add faint lines for veins in the skin.

Use an eraser to remove any unwanted construction lines.

19

Werewolf

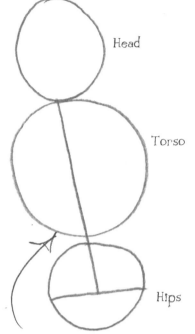

Beware the full moon! Once this lunar phase is entered, these unassuming cursed people transform into creatures that are half—man and half—wolf, and will tear their victims apart!

Head

Torso

Hips

Sketch an oval for the head and two circles for the torso and hips. Add a centre line for the spine and a line for the hips.

Add lines for the arms with circles for the joints.

Add circles for the hands.

Draw short lines for the legs.

Draw circles to indicate joints.

Add two large flipper—like feet.

Position the ear and eye.

Sketch in construction lines for the shape of the snout.

Add claws to the hands.

Join the head to the shoulders.

Finish the snout details and add sharp teeth.

Sketch on the ripped trousers.

Join the torso to the hips

Draw on the limbs using the construction lines as a guide.

Draw lots of short lines to indicate the fur.

Add the shape of the tail.

Complete the hands, adding pads and claws.

Add claws to the feet.

Finish the furry tail.

Complete the torn and ragged trousers.

Remove any unwanted construction lines with an eraser.

Draw in the details of the elongated feet.

21

Ghost

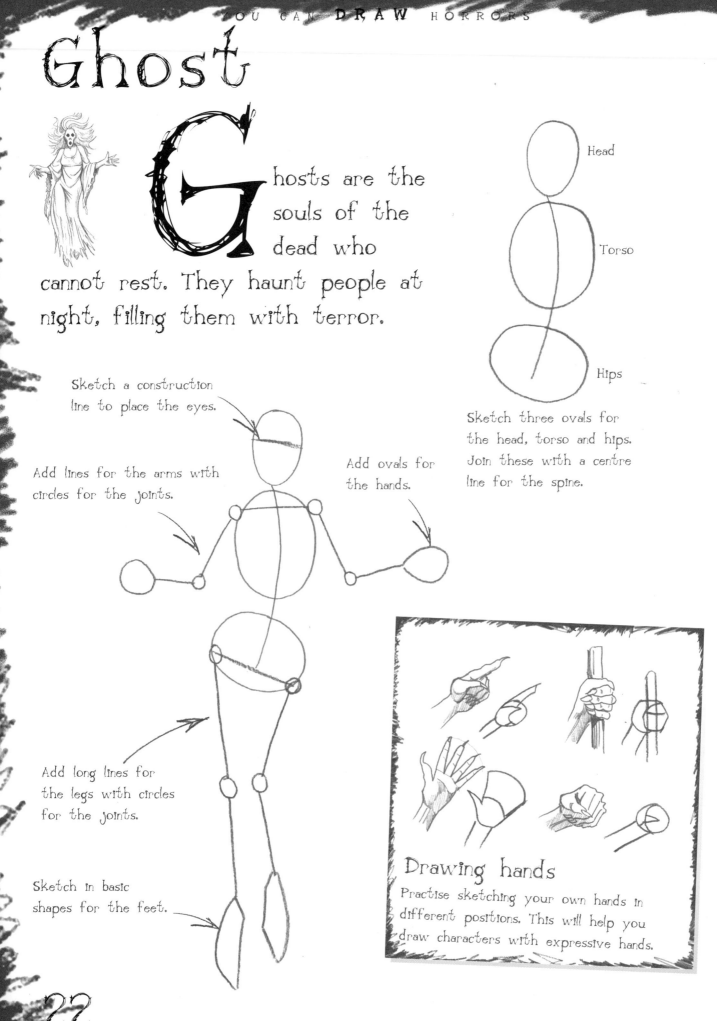

Ghosts are the souls of the dead who cannot rest. They haunt people at night, filling them with terror.

Head

Torso

Hips

Sketch three ovals for the head, torso and hips. Join these with a centre line for the spine.

Sketch a construction line to place the eyes.

Add lines for the arms with circles for the joints.

Add ovals for the hands.

Add long lines for the legs with circles for the joints.

Sketch in basic shapes for the feet.

Drawing hands

Practise sketching your own hands in different positions. This will help you draw characters with expressive hands.

Add pointed fingers.

Sketch in the arms using the construction lines as a guide.

Sketch in curved lines for the shape of the chest.

Add the outline of the body with long curved lines.

Draw dark holes for the eyes, nostrils and mouth.

Add long, wavy lines for the hair.

Draw in the legs using the construction lines as a guide.

Draw lines to show the dress fabric hanging loosely on the figure.

Shade areas where light would not reach.

Add straggly lines to create the ragged sleeves and hemline.

Remove any unwanted construction lines.

Draw in the toes.

Witch

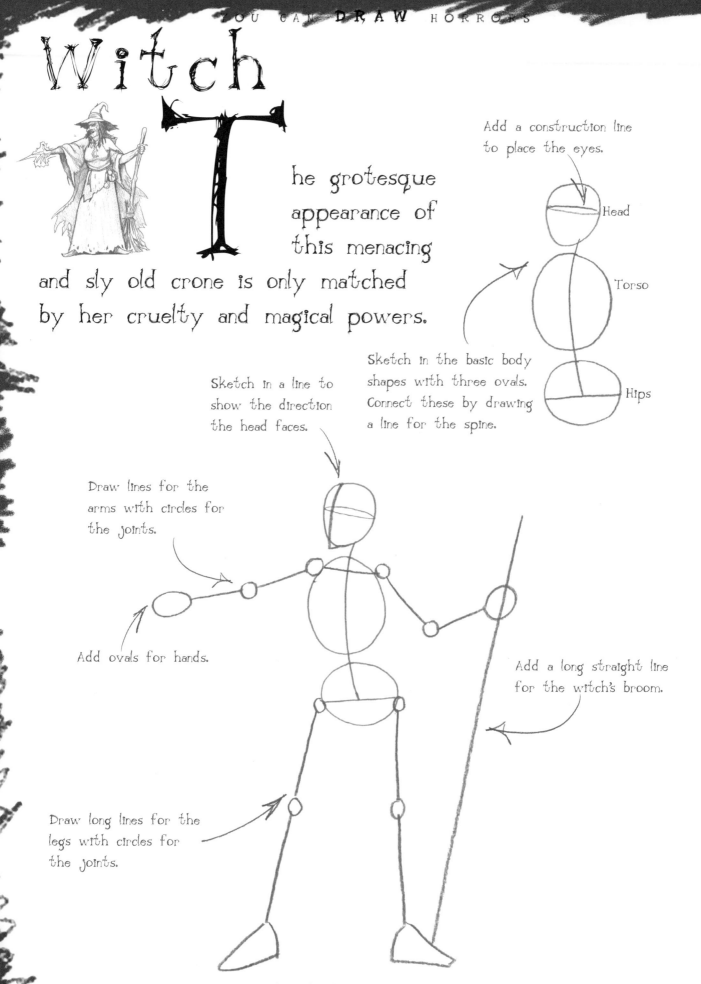

The grotesque appearance of this menacing and sly old crone is only matched by her cruelty and magical powers.

Add a construction line to place the eyes.

Head

Torso

Hips

Sketch in the basic body shapes with three ovals. Connect these by drawing a line for the spine.

Sketch in a line to show the direction the head faces.

Draw lines for the arms with circles for the joints.

Add ovals for hands.

Add a long straight line for the witch's broom.

Draw long lines for the legs with circles for the joints.

Add triangle shapes for the feet.

Draw in the shape of the witch's crooked hat.

Add basic facial features including a long nose!

Draw in the arms using the construction lines as a guide.

Draw this hand grasping the broom.

Add the shape of the broom bristles.

Complete the details and shading of the crooked hat.

Draw long flaring lines for the clothes.

Finish the ugly facial features.

Add ragged edges to her sleeves and clothes.

Draw sharp lines for magic shooting out of the witch's hand.

Add shading to areas where light won't reach.

Add trinkets to the witch's belt.

Add tears and holes to the clothing.

Using an eraser, remove any unwanted construction lines.

Frankenstein's creature

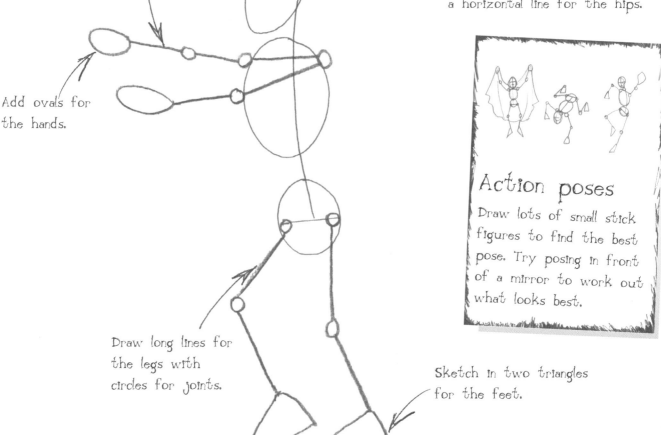

Victor Frankenstein plundered body parts to create an undead being in a terrifying electrical experiment. This man—made creature walks the night alone.

Head

Draw in the position of the eyes

Torso

Hips

Draw two ovals for the head and torso and a circle for the hips. Draw in a centre line and a horizontal line for the hips.

Add lines to draw outstretched arms through the torso. Draw circles for joints.

Add ovals for the hands.

Draw long lines for the legs with circles for joints.

Action poses

Draw lots of small stick figures to find the best pose. Try posing in front of a mirror to work out what looks best.

Sketch in two triangles for the feet.

26

Draw fingers on the hands.

Add basic facial features.

Sketch in the hair.

Add a bolt through the neck.

Sketch in the basic shape of the jacket. Make the sleeves look short.

Add a pocket to the jacket.

Draw the trousers and belt using the construction lines as a guide.

Finish the details of the head.

Add some details to the shoes.

Add shading to areas that light won't reach.

Draw patches on the knee and elbow.

Draw the laces and extra detail on the shoes.

Use an eraser to remove any unwanted construction lines.

27

Scarecrow

This frightening character bursts into life on Halloween, scaring innocent bystanders and terrorising nearby towns.

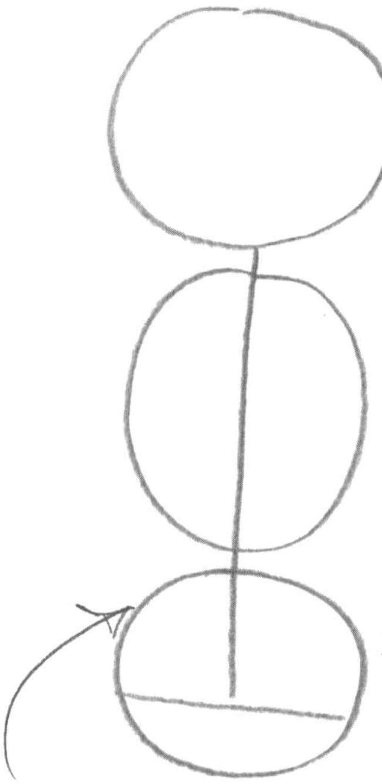

Head

Torso

Hips

Draw two circles for the head and hips and an oval for the torso. Add a curved line for the spine and a horizontal line at the hips.

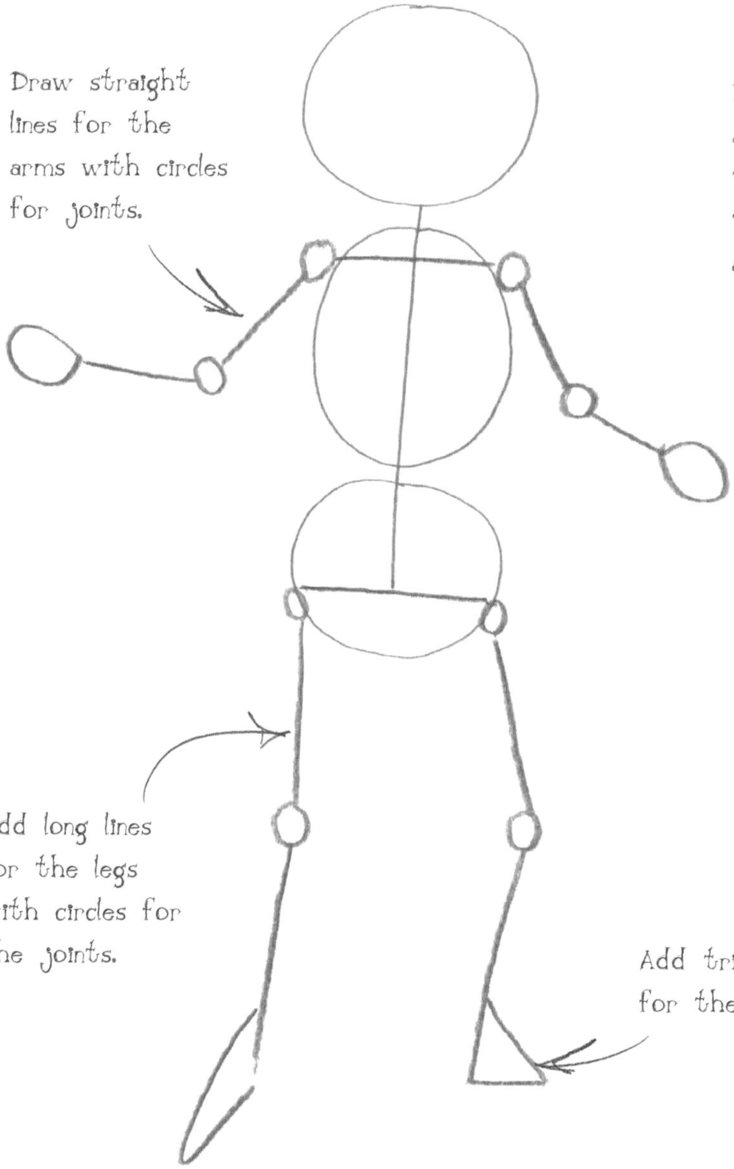

Draw straight lines for the arms with circles for joints.

Add ovals for the hands.

Add long lines for the legs with circles for the joints.

Add triangle shapes for the feet.

Draw in the shape of the pumpkin head. Add its scary features.

Draw in the branch-like shapes for the fingers.

Add the shape of the scarf.

Draw in the ragged shape of the coat using the construction lines as a guide.

Draw a tie-string belt.

Add details to the coat, like tears and patches.

Draw the feet in as spiky branch shapes.

Complete the spiky branch-like hands.

Add shading to areas where light wouldn't reach.

Use jagged lines for the ragged sleeves, trousers and hemlines.

Remove any unwanted construction lines with an eraser.

The Grim Reaper

Hope you don't meet up with this cloaked figure any time soon! His appearance means your life has come to an end, as he has come to collect your soul.

Head

Torso

Hips

Draw in rounded shapes for the head, neck, torso and hips. Add a line for the spine.

Sketch in the construction lines for the facial features.

Draw a long curved line for the scythe.

Draw straight lines for the arms with circles for the joints.

Add ovals for the hands.

Sketch in long lines for the legs with circles for the joints.

Sketch in the shapes of the feet.

Draw the basic skull features.

Draw the shape of the head inside a loose-fitting hood.

Add curved lines for the blade.

Add the long, open sleeves of the cloak.

Sketch in bony fingers holding the scythe.

Add jagged lines for the flowing edges of the cape and the hemline.

Finish the skull details.

Add lines to create the bony feet.

Add shading to areas where light would not reach.

Complete the details of the scythe.

Draw in a pile of skulls and bones.

Add tonal lines for folds in the cloak.

Use an eraser to remove any unwanted construction lines.

31

Glossary

Centre line Often used as the starting point of the drawing, it marks the middle of the object or figure.

Construction lines Guidelines used in the early stages of a drawing, and usually erased later.

Fixative A type of resin used to spray over a finished drawing to prevent smudging. **It should only be used by an adult.**

Perspective A method of drawing in which near objects are shown larger than faraway objects to give an impression of depth.

Pose The position assumed by a figure.

Proportion The correct relationship of scale between each part of the drawing.

Silhouette A drawing that shows only a flat, dark shape, like a shadow.

Vanishing point The place in a perspective drawing where parallel lines appear to meet.

Index